BOOK ANALYSIS

Written by Magali Vienne
Translated by Soline de Dorlodot

Girl with a Pearl Earring

BY TRACY CHEVALIER

TRACY CHEVALIER

AMERICAN NOVELIST

- **Born in 1962 in Washington**
- **Notable works:**
  - *The Virgin Blue* (1997), novel
  - *Girl with a Pearl Earring* (1999), novel
  - *The Lady and the Unicorn* (2003), novel

Tracy Chevalier is an American author who was born in 1962 in Washington. After graduating in English in Ohio, she left the United States to go to the UK, where she has been living since 1984. She first worked in the publishing world, before starting a course in creative writing at the University of East Anglia, during which she published her first work of fiction, called *The Virgin Blue* (1997).

It was with her second novel, *Girl with a Pearl Earring*, that she became truly successful. Since then, she has frequently published historical novels, the most well-known being *The Lady and the Unicorn* (2003) and *Burning Bright* (2007).

GIRL WITH A PEARL EARRING

IT ALL STARTED WITH A PAINTING...

- **Genre:** novel
- **Reference edition:** Chevalier, T., (2001). *Girl with a Pearl Earring*. New York: Penguin Books.
- **1st edition:** 1999
- **Themes:** painting, religion, jealousy, friendship, love

Published in 1999, *Girl with a Pearl Earring* is Tracy Chevalier's second novel. Inspired by a painting by the Dutch painter Johannes Vermeer (1632-1675), it tells the imaginary story of the young unknown woman who sat for this painting. Indeed, up to now, historians still have no information concerning the model of the famous painter.

It is a historical novel written in the first person singular, and tells the story of Griet, a young 16-year-old servant, from the beginning of her service at the Vermeers until the death of the painter.

SUMMARY

In 1664, in Delft, Griet, a young 16-year-old woman, learns that she has been hired as a maid to work for the painter Johannes Vermeer (Dutch painter, 1632-1675), as her family is ruined (an accident cost her father his eyesight, when he was a tiler). Her new masters come to meet her while she is helping her mother with cooking and she leaves her family the next day. Her father gives her a piece of tile on which two children are painted: Griet, and her younger brother Frans.

When she arrives, Griet meets the Vermeer children, who are playing in front of the door, as well as Tanneke, the other servant. Tanneke introduces her to Maria Thins, who is the mother of the painter's wife, Catharina Vermeer, and the real master of the house. She is told what will be expected of her, namely the cleaning of the painter's studio, where all the objects have to be kept in the exact same place they were found. In the afternoon, she goes to the market with Tanneke, who introduces her to the butcher where the Vermeer family buys its meat. This is how Griet meets Pieter, the butcher's son, who will later become her husband. After these encounters, Griet goes to the canal, accompanied by the children, and is bullied by Cornelia, the second Vermeer daughter. Griet slaps her to make it clear that she will not be browbeaten, and then realizes that the young girl might cause her problems.

On Sunday, Griet goes back to her parents' home for dinner and gives them the money she earned during the week. She also meets with her younger sister, Agnes. Unfortunately, a few days later, Griet hears from Pieter that the neighborhood in which her family lives has been struck by the plague and that the authorities are going to order a quarantine. Therefore, Catharina forbids her to go home until the epidemic has officially ended. After several anxious days, Pieter tells her that Agnes is ill. She dies at the end of the summer.

One day, Vermeer, who works with the help of a camera oscura, invites Griet to use it and explains to her how it works. This is the beginning of the complicity between the painter and the young woman. When the painting on which Vermeer has been working since Griet's arrival is finished, he asks the man who commissioned the painting, Mr. Van Ruijven, to visit. Van Ruijven is the painter's biggest client. While he is visiting to have a look at the finished painting, he comes across Griet and is stricken by her charms. On a particularly cold day in January, while the young woman is about to go to the apothecary to get medicine for the children, Vermeer asks her to bring him back ingredients for his colors, a task that he had never entrusted to anyone until then. Cornelia, having heard the exchange, breaks Griet's piece of tile out of jealousy.

A few weeks later, Catharina gives birth to her sixth child. A big dinner is organized to celebrate the event. Pieter comes to deliver the meat at the house. As Griet comes out to welcome him, Vermeer follows her and catches the young butcher's smile. The young woman becomes immediately aware of the tension between the two men. In April, Pieter comes to Griet's church to meet her parents. After that, he is regularly invited to their home on Sundays. A few months later, he tells her that he will ask for her hand in marriage when she turns 18.

The painter asks for Griet's assistance more and more often, even teaching her how to crush the ingredients to make the colors. He does not dare to talk to his wife about how Griet helps him, but manages to get her to agree to have the girl sleep in the attic instead of the cellar, which allows her to work for him very early in the day or in the evening before going to bed.

One day, Maria Thins discovers what Griet does for the painter. She then asks her to do her best to enable him to paint faster, but forbids her to mention her assistance to Catharina or Tanneke. Cornelia, jealous of the interest her father has taken in Griet, decides to make her life a living hell and ambushes her so that Tanneke discovers her collaboration with the artist. Cornelia steals a tortoiseshell comb from her mother and puts it among Griet's belongings, stealing the maid's own comb at the same time. Griet discovers the ploy and mentions it to Vermeer. The painter takes Griet's side and Cornelia is severely punished. The support Vermeer grants to Griet against his own daughter changes the way the other women in the house see her: Tanneke becomes nicer, Catharina's distrust grows, and Maria Thins respects her more.

Vermeer begins a new painting portraying Van Ruijven's wife. Griet, who finds the composition too orderly, takes the liberty of changing the way the tablecloth falls. Surprised, the artist asks her why she made the change and is astonished to learn something from a servant. His respect for her is growing.

Later, Van Ruijven states that he wants to be in a painting with Griet. Worried, Griet refuses and tells of her fears to Maria Thins. Vermeer, to protect the young woman whilst satisfying his most important customer, promises him that he will make a painting of Griet alone. Thus, the young woman sits for the painter. To add a touch of color to the composition, Vermeer wishes her to wear Catharina's pearls. The servant girl does not like the idea of this, but she does not have a choice. While she arranges her hairdo in the storeroom one day, Vermeer climbs up and sees her with her hair down. They are both troubled. Upset that the painter saw her like that, Griet lets Pieter do as he wishes and he has sex with her.

Later, Cornelia discovers that Griet wore the pearls and decides to inform her mother. As proof, she shows her the painting. Catharina has a violent argument with her husband and tries to destroy the painting. Moreover, she accuses Griet of being a thief. Neither Maria Thins nor Vermeer come to her defense. Catharina has a miscarriage in the studio. Deeply shaken by all these events, Griet flees.

A few years later, Griet is married to Pieter and has two children. While she is manning her stand at the market, Tanneke comes to tell her that Catharina wishes to see her. Catharina tells her that Vermeer, who has died, wished her to have the pearls. Griet accepts them and sells them, thinking that the money will serve to pay off the debts that Vermeer still owed the butcher. She does not intend to tell her husband where the money came from.

CHARACTER STUDY

GRIET

Griet is the narrator of the novel. She is a young woman from the working class in Delft, whose parents fell into poverty after her father had an accident that left him blind. Being the eldest, she is placed as a servant to feed her family.

Griet is practical-minded and very meticulous. This is why she is hired at the Vermeers': she is able to place the objects of the studio exactly where she found them after cleaning the room. She also has an artistic feeling: although she does not know anything about the theory of painting, she has a painter's instinct (she unconsciously orders vegetables by color, she changes the fall of a tablecloth to change the composition of a painting, etc.). Tactful, she knows which words to use to avoid problems. She also has a personal ethos.

She is entirely dedicated to Vermeer, even though she is aware of the fact that some of the things he asks her to do will lead to her downfall.

VERMEER

Vermeer is a true artist. Very calm and quiet, he lives in the margin of his household's everyday life: he does not partake in the discussions concerning household matters, leaves Maria Thins to negotiate his contracts, and does not take an interest in the upbringing of his children. He only cares for painting: he does not take into account the consequences this could have on the lives of the other people in his household, including Griet.

Protestant by birth, he converted to Catholicism when he married Catharina. Very much in love with his wife, he is nevertheless troubled by his young maid: he is jealous of Pieter, the butcher's son and does not allow van Ruijven to use Griet for his pleasure, as he would have wished.

CATHARINA

Catharina is Vermeer's wife. Already the mother of five children, she is pregnant with her sixth when Griet comes to work for them. Although at first she seems very self-confident, it becomes clear quite quickly that she is not comfortable with her role as mistress of the house. From the beginning, she sees Griet as a rival: she is soon jealous of the interest her husband takes in her and, most of all, of the trust he grants her. Unlike the young woman, Catharina is not allowed to go in Vermeer's studio, because she is too clumsy.

CORNELIA

Cornelia is the Vermeers' second daughter. She has a changeable nature, like her mother. From the first day, she decides that Griet will be her enemy: throughout her stay with the Vermeers, the girl will make her pay for the slap she received. She is at the source of all the problems Griet will encounter in the house.

MARIA THINS

Maria is Catharina's mother. An old woman with a strong personality, she is the one who governs the house in reality: she manages her daughter's temper, is in charge of the household's finances, negotiates the sale of paintings, etc. She quickly discovers that Griet is not like the other servants: she covers for her several times to allow her to work for Vermeer, and she is the one who gives her the pearls for the portrait. However, she does not hesitate to sacrifice the young maid when Catharina discovers the secret.

TANNEKE

Tanneke has been Maria Thins' servant since she was fourteen. Extremely loyal to her mistress, she is also terribly proud and does not appreciate the interest Vermeer takes in Griet.

VAN RUIJVEN

Van Ruijven is Vermeer's client and a very rich man who has no ethics whatsoever. A womanizer, he has already impregnated a servant and now has his eyes set on Griet, whom he harasses whenever he gets a chance. He wishes to model at her side, but, faced with the painter's categorical refusal, he finally accepts to have only her portrait.

VAN LEEUWENHOEK

Van Leeuwenhoek is Vermeer's closest friend. He does not

appreciate Catharina, who does not like him either. A loyal man, he becomes fond of Griet and does not hesitate to warn her about the artistic madness of Vermeer. He will be the painter's testamentary executor.

PIETER

A young butcher, Pieter falls in love with Griet the moment they meet. A quiet and sweet-tempered young man, he first becomes her friend, before making it clear that he wishes to be something more. He stays patient in the face of Griet's reluctance and waits for her eighteenth birthday to ask for her hand in marriage. Respectful of his fiancée's secrecy, he grants her a relatively great amount of freedom.

ANALYSIS

A HISTORICAL NOVEL

This novel is inspired by a real painting made by Johannes Vermeer in 1665 called *Girl with a Pearl Earring*. Consequently, Tracy Chevalier studied Vermeer's biography and that of his relatives closely, in order to mix real biographic elements into the fictional storyline:

- The paintings described are indeed pieces from Vermeer's body of works: the one for which Tanneke modelled is called *The Milkmaid*, Van Ruijven really modelled for *The Concert*, etc.;
- Vermeer converted to Catholicism;
- Van Ruijven really was Vermeer's client, and van Leeuwenhoek was a scholar who was named curator of Vermeer's debts after his death.

The way the American writer depicts Delft is also close to the historical truth of the city: the importance of earthenware commerce (the city's specialty), the quarantine of some neighborhoods of the city because of the plague, etc.

As the author refers to a real context and characters who really existed, the book can be called a historical novel. The main characteristic of this genre is the mixing of fiction with historic facts. Here, Griet's character and her relationship with the painter are directly issued from Tracy Chevalier's imagination.

THE THEME OF RELIGION

Since the Wester Schism (14th -15th century), the inhabitants of the Low Countries were mainly Protestant. However, a Catholic minority also used to live in the country. This religious duality can be found in Griet's character, as she is Protestant but goes to work for the Vermeers, who are Catholics. The maid had never known Catholics until she began working for the Vermeers , as the two communities did not usually mix. ("They [the Catholics] were tolerated in Delft, but were expected not to parade their faith openly", p. 13).

Griet's discomfort when around the Catholic religion is strongly highlighted in the novel, especially in the first part:

- The author emphasizes Griet's unease when faced with paintings representing the crucifixion;
- The young woman refuses to stay in the house on Sundays, when she is not allowed to go home because of the plague: "I did not want to remain at the house, though—whatever Catholics did on Sundays, I did not want to be among them" (p. 64);
- Griet asks Vermeer about the Catholic nature of his paintings.

However, Tracy Chevalier insists on the respect of the other people's faith: Griet agrees to thank God with the rest of the family at Franciscus' birth.

AN AMBIGUOUS RELATIONSHIP

The whole of the novel is focused on the ambiguous relationship, mixed with respect and unspoken desire, that exists between Vermeer ad Griet.

Griet's feelings towards the painter are specifically noticeable because she never names him, as opposed to the other members of the household, whom she calls by their first names. When she talks about Vermeer, she uses the following words: he, him, my master. She never pronounces his surname, nor his first name.

Similarly, their feelings for each other are never specified: we only know that Griet is troubled by the topic of Vermeer's hands on hers when he teaches her how to crush the ingredients, or by the way he looks at her. We also know, because of a gaze, that Vermeer does not like Pieter, although the word 'jealousy' is never used.

Their relationship remains in the domain of the unspoken and fantasy. For example, Griet thinks of the scene in Vermeer's studio to feel desire in Pieter's arms.

THE SYMBOLISM OF THE HAIR

Hair has a very important meaning in the artistic world. It is often related to modesty and seduction.

Griet always wears a cap, whether at home or outside. This is due to the fact that her hair is very voluminous and unruly, which, according to her, makes her look like "another

Griet—[...] A Griet like the women who dared to bare their heads" (p. 122). Although her relationship with Pieter is quite intimate, she refuses to let him see her hair, afraid that he would have a bad opinion of her and mistake who she is.

The day Vermeer sees her bare-headed in the attic, while she is styling her hair, something snaps in Griet: "Now that he had seen my hair, now that he had seen me revealed, I no longer felt I had something precious to hide and keep to myself" (p. 196). She throws away her modesty with Pieter: they have sex in an alley.

THE IMPORTANCE OF REPETITION

The overall structure of the novel is relatively straight-forward and follows the chronological order of the events. It is divided into four parts: 1664, 1665, 1666, and 1676. The three first parts represent the years Griet spends in the employment of the Vermeer family, and the last part is when she learns of the death of her former master and has to go back to the house of her former employers one last time.

Between the first and the last part, there are many similarities. Indeed, when Griet goes back to the Vermeers, she has the feeling that she is experiencing her first day as a maid again:

- There are four children sitting by order of size in front of the house, with the eldest playing with soap bubbles;
- The children jostle to be the first to tell of Griet's arrival;
- Maria Thins is unchanged. She repeats the same sentence she used to grumble when Griet worked at their place:

"The most trouble we've ever had with a maid" (p. 228);

- The advice Van Leeuwenhoek often gave her is repeated, namely "take care to remain yourself" (p. 232);
- Griet slaps Cornelia like she had done when they first met.

Another main element of the novel is the star on the marketplace, which marks each main stage of Griet's life:

- The day she started working as a maid, she took the way pointed by the eights branch of the star, the one she had never followed before;
- When she flees from the Vermeer's house, she circled the center of the star several times, because she does not know which direction to take;
- After having received Catharina's pearls, she circles the star several times before deciding to sell them.

Finally, one sentence is repeated and marks the step from childhood to adulthood, and the time of disillusions: "only thieves and children run" (p.74 & p. 216).

- The first time, Griet thinks this sentence when she leaves the market running after having heard that the plague has struck her neighborhood: this is the child who wants to see her parents.
- The second time, she leaves the Vermeer's house after having been accused of taking Catharina's pearls. The artistic genius of Vermeer has triumphed, destroying the young woman's innocence.

FURTHER REFLECTION

SOME QUESTIONS TO THINK ABOUT...

- How does Tracy Chevalier's style betray her popular origins? Illustrate your answer with the help of a few examples from the text.
- Griet's father's blindness could be just a minor detail in the story. However, it is a key element in the development of the narration. What does it add to the novel (both in terms of content and form)?
- How does this work symbolize the loss of innocence?
- To what literary genre does it belong? Justify your answer using examples.
- Although Griet and Vermeer's relationship is purely platonic, can it be said that it is sometimes tinted with erotism? Why?
- In her description of the paintings by Vermeer, Tracy Chevalier manages to showcase the characteristics of the artists' style perfectly. What are these characteristics? To which broader painting style do they belong?
- The difference of religion between Griet and her new masters is often discussed in the novel. In your opinion, what message is the author trying to convey? Justify your answer.
- Susan Vreeland (American journalist, born in 1946) took inspiration from another painting by Vermeer, *Girl in Hyacinth Blue* (1999) to tell its story. What are the differences and similarities in the way the two authors retold the story of these two paintings?
- Griet ends her story with the following thought: "I would

not have cost him anything. A maid came free" (p. 233). In your opinion, what does this mean?

- Peter Webber adapted *Girl with a Pearl Earring* (2003) for the screen. What means did he use to create the atmosphere specific to Vermeer's painting, which is so present in the novel?

We want to hear from you!
Leave a comment on your online library
and share your favourite books on social media!

FURTHER READING

REFERENCE EDITION

- Chevalier, T., (2001). *Girl with a Pearl Earring*. New York: Penguin Books.

ADAPTATIONS

- *Girl with a Pearl Earring*, film by Peter Webber, starring Scarlett Johansson and Colin Firth, 2003.